AMERICA'S HOLY WAR

ABSTRACT

This paper examines America's strategic policy to combat terrorism. The paper identifies that the current national strategy is strategically flawed by misidentifying the true enemy the nation faces and that <u>The Global War On Terrorism is a national policy/strategy to combat a "tactic" used by Islamic Extremists vice focusing on the true enemy, the Muslim population that supports this Holy War in the name of Islam.</u>

First, the strategic flaw of the GWOT as a national strategy will be identified followed by an in-depth review of the GWOT. Next, the goals and strategy of Islam and Islamic Extremist are reviewed, and then contrasted to the United States goals. Shortfalls of the United States GWOT policy in combating the Holy War are identified and a new proposed strategy to combat the ideology of Islam and the Muslim support base is provided. A short case study to demonstrate the ramifications of appeasement and misidentifying the strategic enemy is incorporated for historical reference.

Table Of Contents

Chapter 1.

Introduction

This paper will examine America's strategic policy to combat terrorism. The current national strategy is strategically flawed by misidentifying the true enemy the nation faces. <u>The Global War On Terrorism (GWOT) is a national policy/strategy to combat a "tactic" used by Islamic Extremists vice focusing on the true enemy, the Muslim population that supports this Holy War in the name of Islam.</u>

By conducting an overview study of the religion of Islam and the Muslim culture and mindset, it will become apparent that not only is the majority of the Muslim world population supporting the violent extremist movement, but that this violence is a reoccurring event in the history of Islam. The GWOT's strategic flaw of misidentifying the strategic enemy and the ramifications of that action will be further identified and discussed. A short case study to further demonstrate the ramifications of appeasement and misidentifying the strategic enemy will also be provided.

A comparison of Islamic and United States goals and strategies will provide a better understanding of the real strategic threat facing the United States. This in turn will provide the framework for accurately identifying the enemy's Center Of Gravity (COG) and lead to a new proposed national strategy on how to better combat/neutralize the Holy War taking place between the United States and the religion of Islam supported by the Muslim population.

Chapter 2.

Identifying the strategic flaw of GWOT as a National Strategy to counter Islamic Extremists and Islam

The United States of America is involved in a "Holy War" with the followers of Islam, but fails to acknowledge the fact or understand the strategic threat. Instead, the United States administration has adopted a policy that focuses on terrorism and Islamic Extremists. The Global War On Terrorism is a National policy/strategy to combat a "tactic" used by Islamic Extremists vice focusing on the true enemy, the religion of Islam and the Muslim population that supports this Holy War.

The current administration has repeatedly stated that the United States is not at war with Islam and that the majority of the Muslim population is peaceful, and not supporting of these terrorist actions taking place around the world today. Further, the current policy states that it is the act of only a small part of the Muslim population that is waging this war of terror, identifying this small body as Islamic extremists, who manipulate the teachings of the Qur'an to justify their actions of war. Though true in fact that only a small number of Islamic extremists are conducting the actual fighting, they benefit from the support of Muslim populations around the world. This support includes finance, ideology, safe havens, education, recruitment grounds, and acceptable social tolerance for terrorism and violence.

It is understandable why the United States refuses to admit or recognize the fact that they are involved in a Holy War with Islam. First, the religion of Islam is the fastest growing religion in the world. With an estimated 1.6-1.79 billion followers,[1] it is forecasted that by 2025 more than one third of the world's population will be Muslim.[2] To acknowledge that the United States is at war with a large population of the world poses a dilemma never faced before by this nation. The implications of facing such a challenge are almost overwhelming and not desired by the United States government. Second, it is almost incomprehensible to this nation, founded upon the principle of freedom of religion, that any religion would declare war on her. The United States views itself as a good and fair nation and does not understand the deep-rooted hatred that prevails in the Muslim world towards it.

The Muslim world is a vast, diversified mix of civilizations. To generalize about such a complex religious community is very challenging; however, as Thomas Friedman points out, "one need only look at the headlines in any day's newspaper to appreciate that a lot of anger and frustration seems to be bubbling over from the Muslim world in general and from the Arab-Muslim world in particular."[3] The belief that the majority of the Muslim population is supporting this Holy War is based on several issues stemming from the Arab-Muslim population in particular. The United States association with Israel and the Arab-Israeli conflict has spawned an entire generation of Arab-Muslims that now view the United States with equal hatred as they do Israel. Religious beliefs and differences are another issue that adds Muslim support. Yet, these are not the main issues that foster the largest number of Muslim supporters. Rather, the larger issue is one of frustration and humiliation.

The frustration comes from several sources, to include living under authoritarian governments and stifling religious restraints. These bodies limit the opportunities available to their population in both modern education and jobs. The vast majority of the Muslim population has little to no voice in their own future, living under the constraints placed upon them by their religion. The frustration is magnified by the knowledge that a large majority of the non-Muslim world is living a better life with more freedoms and choices of self-determination. Rapid growth of media and internet resources constantly provides images of western life that are impossible to ignore by the more deprived Muslim populations. Raised to believe that Islam is the most perfect and complete expression of Allah's monotheistic message, Muslims cannot vent this frustration at their own religion; rather, this frustration is vented at the West, focusing on the belief that Western decadence is a mortal sin according to Islam.

The Arab-Muslim frustration also breeds humiliation. The humiliation felt by the Arab-Muslim population is derived from their inability to compete with the modern world. Restricted by their religion and culture, Muslims are unable to express critical thought or original thinking in many fields without fear of reprisal. Thomas Friedman surmises, "When you take the economic and political backwardness of much of the Arab-Muslim world today, add its past grandeur and self-image of religious superiority, and combine it with the discrimination and alienation these Arab-Muslim males face when they leave home and move to Europe, or when they grow up in Europe, you have one powerful cocktail of rage."[4]

The combinations of these issues result in the large number Muslims who support the Holy War with the United States. The reactions of the world's Muslim population after 9/11 clearly demonstrate their approval of violence against America. Thomas Friedman recalls, "many Arabs and Muslims were celebrating the idea of putting a fist in America's face-and they were quietly applauding the men who did it. They were happy to see someone humiliating the people and the country that they felt was humiliating them and supporting what they saw as injustice in their world- whether it is

America's backing of Arab kings and dictators who export oil to it or America's backing of Israel whether it does the right things or the wrong things."[5] With few exceptions, mostly out of Spain, Muslim scholars and clerics have remained silent, issuing no fatwa condemning Osama bin Laden for the actions on 9/11. Muslims must understand that by not openly condemning these violent actions, they are consenting by silence and encouraging continued violence through this silent support.

In a government like that of the United States, where religion is separate from the state, it is difficult to comprehend that the United States is involved in a Holy War with the religion of Islam. The easy way out is to blame just a few extremist vice the entire Muslim population. However, like Germany in WWII, it was not just the Nazi Party the United States was at war with, but the whole German population. The Nazi Party led the violence but had the full support of the German nation, just like the Muslim population supports the Islamic Extremists. Until the United States admits this fact and adopts a policy to battle the Muslim support of the Islamic Extremists, the GWOT will never end in victory.

Chapter 3.

The current United States policy/strategy/goals on GWOT

Shifting/evolving US Policy

Since 9/11, the United States President has slowly progressed in clearly defining the enemy in the GWOT. His initial focus on the term of "terrorists" has slowly evolved to "Islamic Extremists" and "Islamic Radicals," yet still remains short of naming the religion of Islam and the Muslim population as accomplices. The most recent National Military Strategic Plan for the War on Terrorism released in February 2006 again fails to identify or associate Islam and the Muslim population of the world as the threat. Extremist organizations, networks, and individuals are identified as the enemy and bear the focus of United States National Military Strategy. The United States continues on the path of failing to correctly identify and engage the true enemy.

US National Strategic Framework for the GWOT

The current United States National Security Strategy drives the strategic framework for the GWOT. This can best be examined by focusing on the **Ends**, **Ways**, and **Means** of the strategy. The **Ends** or overall goal is to preserve and promote the way of life of free and open societies based on the rule of law, the defeat of terrorist extremism as a threat to that way of life, and the creation of a global environment inhospitable to terrorist extremists.[6] This goal defines the national objectives that need to be achieved to ensure the nation's vital interest and way of life.

The **Ways** to this goal focuses on three broad actions. The first action is to protect the homeland. This includes not only strengthening Federal Agencies that operate within the United States in both prevention and reaction, but also supporting them with legal statures to actively pursue and stop terrorists within United States borders. The second action is to disrupt and attack terrorist networks wherever they exist. As stated by President Bush, "Our doctrine is clear: We will confront emerging threats before they fully materialize. And if you harbor a terrorist, you're just as guilty as the terrorist."[7] The third action is to counter ideological support for terrorism. By "motivating Muslims toward the future and not towards a past of confrontation and violence,"[8] the support of violent ideology can be avoided. This action makes the assumption that the GWOT is against Islamic extremism and not against Islam or the Muslim population.

The **Means** available to this strategy are all the instruments (elements) of national power. These instruments consist of Diplomatic, Informational, Military, and Economic (DIME) categories of national power and resources. Developing and employing these instruments of national power in a synchronized and integrated fashion are key factors in achieving national objectives.

Included in this "means" is the ability of the United States to incorporate partners, allies, and international organizations and their respective instruments of power in the support of the GWOT. The addition of these bodies and their respective instruments of power further assist the United States in achieving the outlined goals and capitalize on the **G**lobal in the GWOT. By engaging the enemy across the full spectrum of DIME, this strategy attempts to harness the full power of this nation and focus its resources toward a common goal.

The United States National Security Strategy is the guiding framework for the nation's GWOT (Figure 1.). The failure to correctly identify the true enemy in this Holy War permeates from that document throughout the rest of the nation's strategies, to include the National Military Strategic Plan for the War on Terrorism. Failure to identify or associate Islam and the Muslim population of the world as the threat limits the ability of this nation to bring to focus the instruments of national power, DIME, in an efficient and decisive manner. Until the United States administration adopts a policy to battle the Muslim support of the Islamic Extremists and the Islamic ideology, the GWOT will continue to drain the nation's resources without resolution.

Figure 1.[9]

Chapter 4.

Definitions and Terms: A Prerequisite to Understanding Islam

"Not until terms and concepts have been defined can one hope to make any progress in examining the question clearly and simply and expect the reader to share one's views."[10]

In order to understand the dilemma facing the United States, the terms and definitions of the factors involved must be defined. Many of these factors cross cultures, religions, and nations and therefore have different meanings to each. The following is a brief description and definition of many of the terms as understood and used in this paper by the author to provide a fundamental baseline of understanding. This baseline is critical to comprehending the context of this paper, and is therefore incorporated into the text vice submitted in a glossary.

Allah: The Arabic word for God.

Extremist: Those who (1) oppose—in principle and practice—the right of people to choose how to live and how to organize their societies and (2) support the murder of ordinary people to advance extremist political purposes.[11]

Fatwa: Muslim authoritarian answer to an Islamic legal question or issue posed by a fellow Muslim.

Holy War: A war or violent campaign waged by religious partisans to propagate or defend their faith.[12]

Ideology: A systematic body of concepts especially about human life or culture. It can be thought of as a comprehensive vision, as a way of looking at things.[13]

Islam: A religion based on the final statement of Allah's guidance to mankind revealed through the Prophet Muhammad; literally, submission to God.

Islamic Extremist: A Muslim who uses terrorism in the name of Allah or Islam.

Jihad: Earnest striving or effort, either within oneself, in society, or in the world at large, for righteousness and against evil and oppression. Frequently mistranslated to mean "holy war", although can apply to warfare. It is a struggle against all that is perceived as evil in the cause of that which is perceived as good.

Kafir: Infidel or non Muslim. Possesses a derogatory connotation.

Madrassa: A building or group of buildings used for teaching Islamic theology and religious law.

Muhammad: Prophet of Allah. He is the transmitter of the words of Allah. He is revered but not worshipped by the Muslim population.

Muslim: Anyone who submits to Allah by following Islam.

Qur'an: The divinely-revealed scripture of Islam. Considered sacred by Muslims, both physically and in ideology.

Surah: A chapter in the Qur'an.

Terrorist: People who conduct terrorist acts; use violence and terror tactics against others, especially noncombatants.

Zakat: Almsgiving, obligatory for all Muslims. 2.5% of a Muslims annual income. Spending of these funds is at the discretion of the senior Islamic representative.

Chapter 5.

Islam's and the Islamic Extremists' strategy and goals in their "Holy War"

The goals of Islam and the Islamic extremists share many common threads. Though less publicized outside the Muslim community, Islam's goals can be found clearly stated in the Qur'an. A primary Islamic goal is world dominance by their religion. More obvious and publicized are the goals and strategies of the Islamic Extremist. These goals and strategies can be examined in several published documents and are founded on verses from the Qur'an. An understanding of both goals and strategies is instrumental in understanding that the violence of the Islamic Extremist is just an extension of the Islamic strategy. It is clear that the US administration does not understand the inherent violence within the religion of Islam as demonstrated by President Bush's address to Congress when he stated "Its teachings are good and peaceful, and those who commit evil in the name of Allah blaspheme the name of Allah."[14]

Islam

The religion of Islam is a totalitarian ideology that seeks to use the Qur'an as a vehicle to power. The totalitarian ideology of Islam requires the subordination of the individual to the religion and strict control of all aspects of the life and productive capacity by coercive measures. Islam is not a religion of love and tolerance towards those outside the faith, but rather it is a religion of formally structured rules and beliefs that demand violence and death to all non-believers of Islam. Allah encourages the Muslims throughout the Qur'an to "fight them until there is no persecution and the religion is Allah's." (Surah 2:193) It is the duty of all Muslims to support this effort to ensure that Islam is the prevailing religion in the world. He further clarifies that the enemy of Islam and target of this violence is anyone not following the faith of Islam: "Fight those who believe not in Allah nor the Last Day." (Surah 9:9)

Following these teachings from the Qur'an, one can easily understand why the Islamic faith has used Holy Wars and Jihad for over one thousand years to conquer in the name of Allah. Dr. Ergun Caner points out, "war is not a sidebar of history for Islam; it is the main vehicle for religious expansion. It is the Muslim duty to bring world peace via the sword."[15] The holy war now taking place will only be completed in the eyes of Islam when the entire world is placed under the submission of Allah and when his laws reign supreme.

The Qur'an demands the expulsion or destruction of all kafir (infidels). Complete eradication of the nonbeliever is repeatedly justified throughout the Qur'an. Islam has the distinct characteristic to ideologically legitimize any action that supports the spreading of the religion. The following chapters from the Qur'an are further examples of the Islamic plan for establishing Islam as the sole religion on earth:

> "If anyone desires a religion other than Islam, it will never be accepted of him." (Surah 3:85)
> "For the Unbelievers are open enemies to you." (Surah 4:101)
> "Seize them and slay them wherever you find them: and in any case take no friends or helpers from their ranks." (Surah 4:89)
> "Fight those who believe not in Allah nor the last day." (Surah 9:29)

There are over one hundred verses in the Qur'an that exhort Muslims to wage Jihad against unbelievers.

There are those who continue to defend Islam as a peaceful and tolerant religion. Their defense is continually based on verses from the Qur'an that foster tolerance and peace. They blame fundamentalist for distorting passages from scripture to justify their

Islamic violence. But this 'distortion' could be better clarified as 'interpretation'. Interpretation of the Surahs and actions conducted as the result of these interpretations can only be judged right or wrong by Allah in the Muslim faith. Additionally, the Qur'an fosters many verses that contradict each other or leave interpretation blatantly open to the reader. Additionally, the majority of verses in the Qur'an that foster tolerance and peace are directed at other Muslims, not Kafirs. If by chance these less violent verses are directed at others than Muslims, it will most always include the phrase or concept of submission of the offending party, either through tax or reduction in class status, to the Muslims.

The goals of Islam are clearly stated and a repeated theme in the Qur'an. Through support of Islamic extremists and backed by the world Muslim population, the Holy War to spread Islam and make it the sole religion on earth is well underway and documented.

Islamic Extremists

The declared Islamist Jihadist movement is global expansionism executed by Islamic extremists supported by Islam and the world's Muslim population, not just the defense of the established Islamic world. Its goal is to subdue the House of War, those lands not under Islamic rule, meaning the entire non-Muslim world. Islamic extremists constantly project the misleading concept that reestablishing the historical Caliphate (Figure 2) is their endstate. In reality, reestablishment of the historical Caliphate is only one step in the quest of Islam and the Islamic extremists. In most published documents released by the Islamic extremists, one will see that their true endstate is aligned with that of Islam: a world under Islamic law and rule.

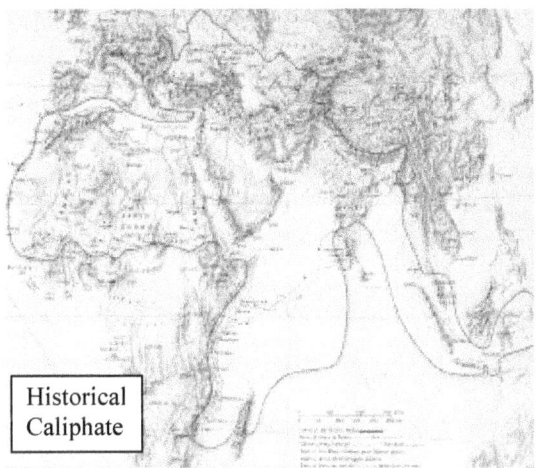

Figure 2. Historical Caliphate

Ayatollah Ruhollah Khomeini is one of the most notable Islamic extremists. His rise to power in Iran in 1979 was instrumental in introducing Islamic extremism into the modern world of politics. Under Khomeini's rule, the strict Shia Islamic law was instituted throughout Iran. Any opposition to his religious rule or Islam in general was met with harsh punishment and retributions. Torture, intimidation, and prison were accepted as legitimate means of enforcing Islamic law under this new regime. Khomeini began to encourage similar Islamic revolutions across the region. His militant brand of Shiism supported the return to strict Islamic law by any means, to include open conflict, assassinations, and terrorist tactics.

Khomeini's extremist views and actions lead to regional insecurity. The Iranian hostage crisis and the decade long Iran-Iraq war are two examples. These events firmly demonstrated the conviction of an Islamic government and its resolve to sacrifice lives for their religion. As leader of the first modern Islamic republic, Khomeini further condoned violence as acceptable in the spread of Islam as illustrated in his fatwa of 1989 in which he wrote, "This fatwa rules the killing of Salman Rushdie a religious necessity for Muslims, because of blasphemy against the prophet Muhammad."[16] Rushdie had written a book, Satanic Verses, which questioned the integrity of the Qur'an, and was therefore sentenced to die by Khomeini. This fatwa not only made it legal and a necessity for all Muslims to kill Rushdie, but it implied it acceptable under Islamic law to administer the same punishment of death to anyone who offended Islam or Muhammad. Khomeini's fatwa set the example and established the foundation of justifying violence against civilians in the name of Islam that would be adopted and mimicked by future Islamic extremists.

This public demonstration of justifying murder in the belief of Islam increased Khomeini's popularity and power not only in the region, but to Muslims worldwide. Testament to Khomeini's influence and popularity was his being named Time Magazine's "Man of the Year" in 1980 and the presence of more than a million Iranians at his burial in 1989.

One of the most publicized fatwa's is the World Islamic Front Statement: Jihad Against Jews and Crusaders, released on February 23, 1998. This fatwa demonstrates several key issues in understanding the beliefs and strategy of the Islamic extremists, as well as offer insight into their conviction. After reading this fatwa in its entirety, there can be no doubt that the Islamic population of the world has been charged with the duty of waging war on the US.

The first key issue of this fatwa is to note the originators and signers of the document:

Shaykh Usamah Bin-Muhammad Bin-Ladin

Ayman al-Zawahiri, amir of the Jihad Group in Egypt
Abu-Yasir Rifa'I Ahmad Taha, Egyptian Islamic Group
Shaykh Mir Hamzah, secretary of the Jamiat-ul-Ulema-e-Pakistan
Fazlur Rahman, amir of the Jihad Movement in Bangladesh

These individuals represent the diversity of sects and nationalities that encompass the Islamic extremist movement. They further demonstrate the willingness of Muslims to put aside their differences to combat a common enemy. These men additionally are extremely popular in their respective regions and among Muslims and represent the Islamic struggle against the US. Bin-Ladin and Zawahiri both embody what the Islamic world views as heroes and leaders of the Islamic movement.

The World Islamic Front Statement identifies and discusses "three facts" that offer keen insight into the beliefs of the extremist. These "facts" are stated to be "known to everyone, and listed in order to remind everyone."[17] It is these "facts" that the Islamic extremist use as their foundation to wage war on the United States. Though open to debate in the eyes of the United States, these "facts" are what is taught in Muslim societies and how the Muslim world views United States involvement in the Middle East.

The first "fact" points out to the readers that the United States has been occupying the lands of Islam for over seven years at the release of this document. The reader is reminded that this occupation is against the desires of the rulers of the territories, humiliates the people, and terrorizes the neighboring states. Reasons for this occupation include plundering and establishing bases to fight neighboring Muslim peoples. The extremists' strategy here is to establish a regional bond between Muslims over the physical conquest of the United States.

The second "fact" states that the United States was not content with the death of over one million Iraqis in the first Gulf War, and is trying to once again repeat the horrific massacres. The reader is warned, "so here they come to annihilate what is left of this people and to humiliate their Muslim neighbors."[18] The goal of publishing this statement is to clearly point out to the Muslim population that the United States desires to kill Muslims. It further appeals to their sense of Islamic brotherhood and attempts to instill the concept that it is the United States against all Muslims.

The third "fact" reiterates that the United States is also trying to divert attention away from Israel's occupation of Jerusalem and the murdering of Muslims there. It further states that one of the United States' goals is to weaken any Islamic state in the region that might threaten Israel's survival. By linking United States intentions in the Middle East with Israel, the extremist are appealing to the deep rooted hatred of Jews by Muslims created over the establishment of Israel and the displacement of the Palestinians.

The authors of this fatwa surmise that the aforementioned "facts" are a clear declaration of war on Allah, his messenger, and Muslims by the Americans. Based on these established "facts" and the precedence established by Khomeini's 1989 fatwa, the following order was issued in the World Islamic Front Statement;

> On that basis, and in compliance with Allah's order, we issue the following fatwa to all Muslims:
> The ruling to kill the Americans and their allies—civilians and military— is an individual duty for every Muslim who can do it in any country in which it is possible to do it, in order to liberate the al-Aqsa Mosque and the holy mosque [Mecca] from their grip, and in order for their armies to move out of all the lands of Islam, defeated and unable to threaten any Muslim. This is in accordance with the words of Almighty Allah, "and fight the pagans all together as they fight you all together," and "fight them until there is no more tumult or oppression, and there prevail justice and faith in Allah." [19]

The Islamic extremists' strategy is clearly outlined in this fatwa. That their goal is to identify the United States with Israel, portray the United States as world aggressors towards Islam and all Muslims, and unite all Muslims in a Jihad against the U.S is surmised in their closing statement where they call on every Muslim who believes in Allah to kill the Americans wherever and whenever they find them. The World Islamic Front Statement: Jihad Against Jews and Crusaders is a clear indication and example demonstrating that ideological differences between Arab nationalist and Islamists will not preclude alliances against a common foe.

The next document examined in this chapter is A statement from qaidat al-jihad regarding the mandates of the heroes and the legality of the operations in New York and Washington. This translated document was released by al-Qaeda on 24 April, 2002 in response to the world outcry about the 2752 civilian deaths on 9/11. The document provides further examples of the mindset of the extremists and their strategic Information Operation techniques. Additionally, it describes and justifies their beliefs that targeting civilians in the name of Islam is not only acceptable, but it is instrumental in the Holy War against the United States. Though written by Islamic extremist, the document gives insight into their rationale and provides assurances for mainstream Muslims to conduct acts of violence.

The initial paragraphs of the document explain that the attacks on the World Trade Centers and the Pentagon were more than justified by the beliefs of Islam. Multiple references are made as to how the United States and its coalitions have been killing and waging war against Islam and Muslims around the world for many decades. The Islamic extremists restate the atrocities conducted against the Palestinians by the Jews, condoned and protected by the United States. Further examples cited include American alliances with Serbia allowing the annihilation of Bosnian and Herzegovina Muslims. The persecution and deaths of Muslims in Kashmiri, Iraq, Afghanistan,

Somalia and the Philippines are all blamed on the United States in its further endeavor to wage war on Islam. The underlying theme of the Islamic extremists justification for 9/11 is that the United States started the Holy War first.

> We must state that all the Muslim peoples whom the worldwide Zionist Crusade has annihilated did not commit any crime except to say, "Allah is our Lord." The Zionist Crusade coalition does not need directives or guilty verdicts against Muslims to begin its war or to continue it. It did not stand around with its hands tied previously, waiting for excuses to launch its wars of extermination against Muslims.[20]

In further understanding the value of human life and mindset of the Islamic extremist, there are several paragraphs in the document rationalizing their targeting civilians. Women, children, and the elderly are referred to as "innocents" or the "protected ones" in the Qur'an. The Islamic extremists list seven conditions in which they view it is permissible to kill humans in this category.

The first condition is one of reciprocity. If Muslim women, children, and elderly are killed by unbelievers, it is permissible for Muslims to respond in kind. The document cites Palestinian cities as an example by stating, "Every day, all can follow the atrocious slaughter going on there with American support that is aimed at children, women, and the elderly. Are Muslims not permitted to respond in the same way and kill those among the Americans who are like the Muslims they are killing? Certainly!"[21]

The second condition is when the killing happens incidentally. If the "protected ones" are among the unbelievers in a stronghold, or one is unable to differentiate the two, it is acceptable to kill them.

The third condition is when the "protected ones" have assisted in combat. Assisted is further defined as deed, word, mind, or any other form of assistance.

The four condition exists when the need to <u>burn strongholds or fields</u> of the enemy so as to weaken them in order to conquer at a later time. If "protected ones" die in these fires, it is acceptable and justified.

The fifth condition allowing the killing of the "protected ones" is while <u>utilizing heavy weapons</u>. The justification for this is that the weapon cannot distinguish between combatants and "protected ones." The document references the historical use of catapults, but it immediately raises the images of Weapons of Mass Destruction (WMD). Under this condition, the use of a WMD in a heavily populated urban environment and the associated massive loss of civilian life would be considered acceptable.

The sixth condition is when the enemy uses the "protected ones" as <u>human shields</u>. It is permissible to destroy the shield to kill the enemy.

The seventh condition condoning the killing of "protected ones" is when they have <u>broken a treaty</u> and must be taught a lesson.

The relevance of these conditions is essential when trying to understand the mind and strategy of the Islamic extremists. The rules and conditions they established for identifying targets are so broadly defined and open to interpretation that virtually anyone can be justifiably targeted under their beliefs. It should also be noted that only one of the seven mentioned conditions must apply to justify the killing of the "protected ones" and that the dissenter has the authority to make that decision. Additionally, each of these conditions are directly traced back to and referenced to a chapter out of the Qur'an.

The document further recognizes that Muslims were killed in the World Trade center attacks as well, and spends several paragraphs justifying their deaths. Again, the document goes into great detail explaining when the killing of Muslims is permissible.

Seven views are outlined defining these actions, and are similar to those conditions governing the killing of the "protected ones."

The first view is based on determining that the one conducting the killing is in fact a Muslim. If the justifications are similar or tantamount to a state of emergency, then the killing is permitted.

The second view is based on the opinion of the majority of the aggressors that only unbelievers were present in the targets that were attacked. If Muslims were present, it was not the attackers' fault if the majority of them did not know of the Muslim presence.

The third view states it is permissible to attack and destroy a country of those who make war on Islam, even if Muslims might be killed by the attack. Holding back from targets that contain Muslims would lead to an interruption in the jihad, and therefore the killing is allowed.

The fourth view further expands the third view's limits of killing Muslims in the world's current situation of Islamic Jihad. The rational being that there are large number of Muslims living in all warring nations that Islamic Jihad is being conducted against. The Jihad must go on despite the loss of these Muslims.

The fifth view refers to the Muslim custom of paying blood money for killing a fellow Muslim living among a warring people. This view removes the blood money custom because in the current Jihad, the custom is too obscured to apply.

The sixth view condones the killing of a fellow Muslim if he has assisted or strengthened the unbelievers. It is at the discretion of the dissenter to make that decision, but the eternal judgment will be decided by Allah in heaven based on the Muslim's true intentions.

The seventh and final view attempts to justify evil actions conducted and condoned in the cause of the Jihad. In simplistic terms, the evil act conducted should not lead to an evil equal to or greater than the act. In conjunction, the evil act should not lead to the suppression of a good equal to or greater than the good caused by the evil act.

The reoccurring theme in killing fellow Muslims during Jihad is that if the action was unwarranted or not justified, Allah will welcome the slain Muslim into heaven and not judge the dissenter. Perhaps this is the Islamic version of the saying, "kill them all and let God sort them out." At the very least, it clearly demonstrates the low regard the Islamic extremist have for human life, regardless of religion or beliefs.

The final statement in the document is a warning to Muslim and Arabs around the world not to denounce these Jihadist attacks or label them criminal. That by doing so only encourages more American aggression. The document clearly threatens, "We warn them about apostasy because of their assistance to the Crusaders by word or by their legal rulings to Arab governments that cooperation against terrorism (by this they mean the mujahideen) is lawful. This is defiant apostasy!"[22]

This document, A statement from qaidat al-jihad regarding the mandates of the heroes and the legality of the operations in New York and Washington, clearly demonstrates the strategy and tactics that the Islamic extremists are willing to utilize in their quest to spread Islam. The justified killing of "innocents" and fellow Muslims further identifies the Islamic ideology based on violence inherent in the Qur'an and the religion of Islam.

The final document submitted for examination is the speech given by Osama bin Laden on the eve of the United States 2004 Presidential elections. This speech served two information operational purposes for the Islamic extremists. The first was to weaken the resolve of the American population in the GWOT while simultaneously slandering the leadership of the United States. Osama bin Laden repeatedly fosters the concept that the attacks on America were in retaliation for United States support of the Israeli invasion into Lebanon in 1982. He further states that President Bush is only interested in money and power, and that he is lying to the American public: "Although we have entered the fourth year after the events of 9/11, Bush is still practicing distortion and deception against you and he is still concealing the true cause from you." [23] Osama bin Laden did not obtain his first goal of this information operation as evidenced by President Bush's reelection, but it did fulfill the second purpose.

The second purpose of this speech was to further strengthen the resolve of Muslims to continue their support of the Islamic extremist Jihad and strengthen the established bonds between Muslims and the Islamic extremist. Bin Laden does this by first associating the United States with Israel in combat actions in the Middle East, and then by stressing the words "we" and "our" in his speech: "*We* had not considered attacking the towers, but things reached the breaking point when *we* witnessed the injustice and tyranny of the American-Israeli coalition against *our* people in Palestine and Lebanon-then I got this idea."[24] This speech served to reinforce in the Muslim mind that the United States, in conjunction with Israel, are aggressors into the Middle East who do not care about the lives of Muslims. It further justifies the Islamic extremists' violence as retaliation justified in the defense of Islam and all Muslims.

Wahhabi recruitment and Islamic finances: bridging the goals; instrument of both.

Used as an instrument of recruitment by both Islam and the Islamic extremist is Wahhabism. Wahhabism is the most pervasive revivalist movement in the Islamic world today and bridges the goals of both Islam and the Islamic extremist as well. Originating out of Arabia in the 1700's by the scholar Muhammad ibn Abd al-Wahhab, Wahhabism tends to apply the teachings of the Qur'an in the literal sense. A return to the pure practice of the fundamentals of Islam according to the Qur'an is the foundation of this sect. "In the eighteenth century, Muhammad ibn Saud, founder of the modern-day Saudi dynasty, formed an alliance with Abd al-Wahhab. From that point forward, there has been a close relationship between the Saudi ruling family and the Wahhabi religious establishment."[25] This relationship includes the adoption of Wahhabism as the state religion of Saudi Arabia and instruction in Wahhabism in all government schools, consuming roughly 30 percent of the kingdom's education budget, as well as funding the proselytization of Wahhabism around the world.

This spread of Wahhabism poses a direct threat to United States national security due to the ease with which their beliefs (Wahhabi) can be used to defend and endorse terrorist acts. A common theme of the Wahhabi is "The concept of victimhood at the hands of the West is a staple of their education system and state-supported media, and is often reinforced by Arab governments seeking to project the blame game onto the always available scapegoats."[26] The US cannot accept or afford the Wahhabi as being the voice for Islam. The Wahhabi literal interpretation of the Qur'an has become a central justification for violence and international Jihad around the world. The growth of "more than 2000 schools for educating Muslim children in non-Islamic countries in Europe,

North and South America, Australia, and Asia have been funded wholly or in part by the Saudi government."[27] It is these schools and madrassas, funded under the guise of religious education, that provide vast human resources for recruitment into the Islamic extremist movements.

Further funding for Wahhabi and Islamic extremists comes from Muslims' annual zakat. Zakat is almsgiving which is obligatory for all Muslims and equates to about 2.5 percent of one's annual income. In Muslim based states, these alms are paid directly to the government who, in theory, exercises the distribution of the money to the needy and Islamic charities. Due to oil revenues, "The UN estimates that the Saudi Zakat, the obligatory religious almsgiving equivalent to 2.5% of Muslims' wealth, is about $10 billion per year."[28] Unfortunately, the distribution of this money often ends up deliberately in the hands of Islamic extremist organizations. *The Committee for Support of the Intifada al Quds*, whose charitable activities include financing Hamas suicide operations in Israel,[29] is one such charitable organization that still receives Saudi state zakat even today.

Private Islamic charities and local mosques fulfill this function in western cultures and states, to include the US. The ability to distinguish between legitimate charities and fronts for sinister organizations linked to Islamic extremist groups is extremely difficult. Islamic charities in the United States receive contributions estimated to be in the hundreds of millions of dollars annually from Muslim zakat. Prior to 9/11, three leading Muslim charity organizations, the Holy Land Foundation for Relief and Development, the Global Relief Foundation and the Benevolence International Foundation, reported raising over $21.5 million dollars annually.[30] This is the annual total from just three out of the 248 registered Muslim charities in the United States. In the United States several of these Muslim charities have been shut down since 9/11 due to ties to Islamic extremist groups. Examples of these closures include "The Holy Land Foundation (based in Dallas, Texas, and allegedly linked to Hamas), The Islamic Assembly of North America (based in Ann Arbor, Michigan, and allegedly linked to al Qaeda) and the Saudi Al-Haramain Islamic Foundation (based in Ashland, Oregon and allegedly linked to al Qaeda)."[31] Through the combination of these untraceable Islamic alms and Saudi funded programs, the Wahhabi and associated Islamic extremist groups have a virtually bottomless monetary fund from which to draw from.

Chapter 6.

Fundamental differences between the United States and Islamic goals

There are several major opposing conflicts in the goals of the two warring sides. Further complicating this war between the United States and Islam is that one side is an established, formal government of a nation state with boundaries, while the opposing side is a fragmented religion without sovereign borders, united only in its hatred of the United States as a symbol of the west. The religion of Islam is currently facing additional internal strife in the form of moderates who want to reform the religion to become more functional in the modern world and the fundamentalist who abide by strict compliance with the Qur'an with little to no modern interpretation of its text.

The United States seeks to preserve and promote the way of life of free and open societies based on the rule of law, freedom, and democracy. Islam is in direct conflict with these tenets. Islam accepts the Qur'an as the rule of law; it does not foster free and open societies. All life under Islam is in accordance with and governed by the Qur'an, not subject to laws established by democratic governments. Freedom of choice is considered a conduit for sin under Islam, leading only to unholyness and damnation. Muslims believe that the only choice is the path of Islam and living a life guided by the surahs of the Qur'an. Democracy and democratic governments will all always be associated with the distain of the Western colonization of the eighteenth and nineteenth centuries in the eyes of most Middle Eastern Muslims. Many Middle East and Africa countries were ruled by caricature democratic governments that suppressed Islam and exploited the resources of the region. Not until after World War II when most Westerners were forced out and strong Islamic governments were established did the

Muslim population of the regions feel free. The fear of another historical suppression of their religion and exploitation of their region is deeply rooted in their culture.

Another goal of the United States is to create a global environment inhospitable to violent extremists and all who support them. This goal unintentionally places the United States in direct opposition to the Muslim world population for it is this Muslim population that is providing the extremists and funding their actions. Exacerbating this tension is that most Muslims believe that western colonization of the eighteenth and nineteenth centuries is the reason for their disastrous economies of today. They believe imperialism allowed the infidels to exploit the Middle East and Africa through political, social, and economic control. The rise of Islamic violence occurring throughout the world today does not reflect a new Islamic ideology but merely a renaissance of Islam. As stated by Dr. Caner, the misidentifying of the real threat is still obvious "Though many in the West call these Muslims extremists, they are actually traditionalists. They look to their past with admiration and nostalgia, hoping to reclaim the glory days of Islam."[32] Again, this places the United States' goal of creating a global environment inhospitable to violent extremists and all who support them in direct contrast to Islam's and the extremists' goal of expanding the Muslim empire to its historical significance.

Perhaps the greatest difference in the opposing goals is the disparity in religious tolerance. The United States is founded on religious tolerance as one of its founding principles, as noted in the Constitution. Fundamentally a Christian society, Americans in general have accepted this religious tolerance as a way of life and have desensitized themselves to differences in religious beliefs. What they cannot fathom or comprehend is a religion that endorses the killing of people of other faiths. Religious Islam affords no such luxury as religious tolerance to other religions, and in fact, it dictates that it is the

goal of all Muslims to spread Islam by any means until it is the only religion.

In the eyes of most Muslims, Americans are viewed as Christians. This leads to

another major fracture between the two religions. Those who would argue that God and

Allah are the same being, or that Islam and Christianity are similar in nature, fail to

recognize three major discrepancies in these thoughts.[33] First, to Christians, Jesus is the

son of God. Allah recognizes no son. Second, Christianity preaches to forgive sinners as

Islam preaches to destroy sinners. And finally, Christianity fosters the ideology of "love

all" as opposed to Islam's ideology of "love only Islam." It is this inability of Americans

to understand these differences between the two religions that cause them to fail to

recognize the violence inherent in Islam. Until Americans truly understand the hatred

and contempt that Islam holds for them, they will be unable to recognize Islam as the true

enemy in this war.

Noted author and former Muslim converted to Christianity Dr. Ergun Caner best

describes the goal of Islam, when he says, "Allah's heart is set against the infidel (kafir).

He has no love for the unbeliever, nor is it the task of the Muslim to 'evangelize' the

unbelieving world. Allah is to be worshiped, period. Any who will not do so must be

defeated, silenced, or expelled. The theme is conquest, not conversion, of the

unbelieving world. Allah has called the Muslim to make the name of Allah alone to be

worshiped."[34] This clear insight into the beliefs of Islam leaves no doubt of the Islamic

goal or the severity of methods Muslims will use to achieve it.

A final point that further demonstrates the differences in the religions is the

comparison of Jesus Christ as the Son of God and Muhammad as a prophet of Allah.

Christians believe that Jesus died on the cross and shed his own blood so that people could come to God. "Muhammad shed other people's blood so that his constituents could have political power throughout the Arabian Peninsula."[35] Again, the inherent violence of Islam is propagated throughout its foundation and accepted as rational behavior in Islamic society.

Resolution of this conflict will also be hampered by the established United States policy of "no negotiations with terrorist." In wars between nations, there exists the ability and opportunity to negotiate for peace or conduct talks for conflict resolution. This includes the ability to negotiate conflicts/disputes of all nature, to include religious conflicts. Currently, the United States administration refuses to acknowledge that negotiations are a viable option for resolution conflict when dealing with the Islamic extremists. The dilemma further increases when one contemplates on how and with whom to negotiate when dealing with a fragmented religion like Islam.

Chapter 7.

Identifying the shortfalls of the United States GWOT policy in combating the larger issues associated with the "Holy War"

Failure to clearly identify or define the enemy is the greatest shortfall of the U.S GWOT strategy. The continual redefining and identification by the United States administration to categorize the current enemy is too limited in view to achieve success. Islam is a violent religion that is in direct opposition to the principles of the United States and the American way of life. Ignoring the fact that a Holy War has been declared on the United States and hoping it can be deterred by targeting only a few Islamic extremists is an unrealistic goal or strategy.

The latest publication of the National Military Strategic Plan for the War on Terrorism (NMSP-WOT), released 1 February 2006, again fails to identify that the nation is involved in a holy war. The NMSP-WOT now identifies the enemy as extremists who exploit Islam to attain their ends, inferring that Islam is a victim in the GWOT. Further, it prominently states that the GWOT "is not a religious or cultural clash between Islam and the West..."[36] This blatant attempt to pacify the Islamic population will only be viewed as weakness in their culture and encourage further terrorist attacks. The appeasement of Islamic actions will produce the same results that occurred with Nazi Germany just prior to World War II; that is, it will not stop further violent expansion by the aggressors. The United States did not choose the religion of Islam to be its enemy, they chose us, and ignoring that fact will not make it go away. Acknowledging that the extremists are supported by the Muslim population and legitimized by the religion of Islam is the first step in correcting this shortfall.

Many believe that the majority of the Muslim population does not actively support these terrorist actions. As noted by Colonel De Atkine, "It is incorrect to depict the terrorist acts of the global terrorist against Western, particularly American, targets as unpopular. There is a widespread felling of schadenfreude, a sort of 'they had it coming to them' attitude. As an emotional feeling this should be understood, but not confused with actual support. Between the emotion and the deed there is an immense gap."[37] I would argue that this "gap" is miniscule or even nonexistent. Any population or nation that openly acknowledges these acts of terror as anything other than criminal is just as guilty. Crowds massing in the streets in celebration of successful terrorist bombings are directly contributing to the terrorist cause. They are publicly condoning the actions and, at a minimum, providing the terrorist morale support and further popularity. It is this popularity and support that provides the endless supply of willing terrorists.

Another shortfall of United States policy is spending the majority of its resources (DIME) on physically combating the extremist vice striking at the larger cause and source of the enemy. Although the NMSP-WOT recognizes that "Violent extremist movements can make new terrorists faster than the anti-terror coalition can capture or kill them,"[38] the United States continues focusing its resources on kinetic deterrence options aimed only at a few. The NMSP-WOT identifies that ideological support as the foundation for extremist success and recruitment, but again fails to identify true Islam as the ideology. The willingness of the United States administration to continue down this wrong road will only deplete our nation's resources over time while focusing on the wrong enemy and strategic threat.

The United States' resource allocation to compete with the spread of Wahhabism supported by Islamic funding is another shortfall in the GWOT policy. The continent of Africa provides a good example of the losing battle the United States is facing. The combination of ungoverned space and rampant poverty make this region highly susceptible to the spread of Islam. With the United States currently involved in Afghanistan and Iraq, there are few resources, other than a small JTF, left available to counter the rapid Islamic growth taking place in Africa. Islamic extremists and the Wahhabists both recognize this shortfall and are rapidly filling the void: "A range of Muslims, buoyed by oil-produced wealth, once again believe that Islam can advance into new territories and set up Islamic law."[39]

Similar events are taking place world wide in places like Malaysia and Nigeria as well. The United States must adopt a policy that not only attempts to compete with the Wahhabist for these regions, but she must allocate the resources to counter the Islamic funding.

Chapter 8.

A proposed strategy to combat/neutralize the "Holy War" with Islam and their Muslim support base

To win this Global War On Terrorism, the United States administration needs to make several sweeping changes in their strategy. The first change is to recognize that it is involved in a "Holy War" with Islam and not just a few terrorist networks and organizations. Publicly acknowledging that the majority of Muslims around the world are supporting and condoning these terrorist acts against the West is the first step. The United States must adopt a policy that recognizes Islam as a religion that condones violence and whose goal is a world under Islamic rule. Further, the United States must make it painfully clear that they did not choose this war, however, since it has come, they will hold all Muslims responsible for the continued aggressions. Freedom of religion cannot prevail over freedom of life, and until the Muslim population can control their followers and disavow their acceptance of violence, they will not be immune from scrutiny or protected by the laws that assure religious freedom.

Once the United States has correctly identified the enemy, it will be able to correctly identify and prosecute the enemy's Center Of Gravity (COG). For the purpose of this discussion, we will define COG as "those characteristics, capabilities, or sources of power from which a military force derives its freedom of action, physical strength, or will to fight."[40] The COG for this holy war is the support base provided by the world's Muslim population. The magnitude of this support is almost indefinable, but "support by 1% of the Muslim population would equate to over 12 million people."[41] Though impossible to physically document, the actual number of Muslims who provide this support is almost certainly significantly higher than 1%. This support comes in many forms and could also be identified as the enemy's Critical Capabilities (CC), those things that are considered crucial enablers for the COG. These CC include finance, ideology, safe havens, education, recruitment grounds, and acceptable social tolerance for terrorism and violence. We will examine each of these CC to better understand and define them, then address the Critical Vulnerability (CV) of each and how the United States could counter them.

Finance:

Finance is one of the most tangible and enabling CC of the Muslim support base. Muslims finance their Islamic activities legally and illegally through a variety of tools such as banking, businesses, front companies and charities, wealthy individual backers, state sponsors, criminal activities, and Zakat. Each of these sources combines to produce a virtually unlimited budget for the spread of Islam.

Muslim owned banking institutions and businesses provide multiple services to the Islamic movement. These institutions can legitimately provide funds to the Islamic cause by profits they incur. Saudi Islamic banks play an especially integral part in the distribution of funds to Islamist cells and armed groups scattered throughout the Muslim world: "Former Al Qaeda members have testified that Osama regularly uses the intricate network of Islamic banks and their subsidiaries to bankroll the group's terror activities."[42] Illegitimately, they can launder and transfer funds to violent factions of the Islamic movement. By disguising or erasing records of these distributions of funds, these Islamic banks make it virtually impossible to track down the extremists by following the money.

Front or shell companies and charities are another tool of Islamic finance. These organizations operate under the guise of being a legitimate institution, but in fact are obtaining funds illegally for the Islamic cause. Islamic extremists are using these front companies and banks in conjunction with offshore trusts to hide their assets and protect the identity of individuals, businesses, and other entities they have used to raise money. Despite United States pressures on foreign banks, several countries continue to attract offshore business from Islamic front companies by retaining a liberal "no look" policy.[43]

Establishing international front businesses is a well known and established tool of the Muslim population to support the Islamic extremists. Sudan was home for many years to Al Qaeda owned and operated shell companies. Until their expulsion by the Sudanese government in 1998, Al Qaeda had import-export, investment, and construction shell companies operating in Sudan. Other cases have been documented as well, "In a report submitted to the United Nations Al Qaeda and Taliban Sanctions Committee, the Government of the Philippines indicated that Islamic extremist had established numerous businesses, corporations and charitable institutions there which had served as a network to fund the Abu Sayyaf group as well as other extremist organizations."[44]

Europe is not immune to these front and shell companies either. By establishing a series of shell companies in Switzerland and Italy, Islamic extremists supported by fellow Muslims have been able to protect their transactions and their holdings as well. They are able to avoid or circumvent sanctions by manipulating accounts between front companies and off-shore shell companies. If assets are being scrutinized or questioned by governing authorities, they simply liquidate the accounts electronically to an off-shore bank or transfer the funds to another front company.

Many large and small Islamic charities own and control their own businesses and use them as sources of unregulated funds for use as they please. Several Islamic charity-business networks with links to al Qaeda have been uncovered in the post 9/11 enforcement efforts and investigations. Victor Comras documents, "One such investigation uncovered a number of Saudi and other Middle East businessmen working out of Herndon, Virginia, who had established a network of some 100 intertwined companies and charities directly linked to funding al Qaeda and other terrorist groups."[45] The construct of this network included Islamic charitable organizations as well as businesses and investment firms, some physically real, many purely "paper" organizations.

Criminal activities: The United States and UN resolutions have had some affect on the ability of these Islamic extremist groups's ability to easily move funds from one region to another. Many of these extremist cells have become isolated and are now responsible for much of their own financial support. These cells, now operating autonomously, are raising funds through criminal activities such as the illegal trafficking of drugs, arms, humans, and other stolen contraband. This trend is on the increase as annotated by "The United Nations Monitoring Group received several reports that theft rings which help finance extremist groups, including Al Qaeda cells, have been involved in the trafficking of identify documents and the pilfering of items including computers, cellular phones, passports and credit cards."[46] These Islamic backed crime rings have been reported on the increase and springing up all over Europe to include major organized criminal activities in Spain and Belgium.

The criminal activities surrounding the drug trade business have historically been associated with Islamic extremist groups. The Taliban was reportedly known to receive large percentages from the $6 billion drug trade in Afghanistan. Though it is doubtful that organizations like al Qaeda still benefit directly from Afghanistan drug trafficking, it would conversely make sense that the Islamic extremist group gained great knowledge and point of contacts in the illegal drug trafficking industry. Evidence to support this includes statements from "Mirwais Yasini, the head of Afghanistan's Counter Narcotics Directorate, who maintains that the Taliban and its allies derived more than $150 million from drugs in 2003. He believes that there is still a 'central linkage' between many of the drug traffickers, Mullah Omar, and Osama bin Laden."[47]

Wealthy individual backers and zakat are a major portion of the Muslim population finance support base. With an estimated $80-$90 billion annual oil revenue going into the Saudi government and economy, the funding of Islamic initiatives is well supported. Personal funding provided by individual Muslim backers is virtually untraceable in the Middle East. Bin Laden provides an excellent example of how easily funding can be obtained, "his personal fortune of $300 million derives profits from his own businesses, and his family is worth more than $5 billion."[48] Regardless of his own personal fortune, Bin Laden and other Islamic extremist groups receive funding from the Muslim population where "there are wealthy Muslim dilettantes who contribute lavishly to 'Islamic causes' without caring how the money is spent."[49]

The combination of these sources of funding is estimated to be in the billions of dollars. The result of all these financial conduits is that vast amounts of funds are at the disposal of Islamic extremists and Muslims intent on establishing Islam as the world's sole religion.

Ideology:

Ideology is a critical component of the Islamic movement and helps sustains its other capabilities. Islamic ideology motivates violent actions and inspires Muslims to provide required material resources to conduct the holy war. As discussed earlier, it is the Islamic ideology that condones violence in the name of Allah.

Despite the typology of different sects of Islam, religious fundamentalists "are able to convey their message to both educated and uneducated Muslims, offering a set of themes, slogans, and symbols that are profoundly familiar and therefore effective in mobilizing support in formulating both critique of what is wrong and a program for putting it right" [50] to support their intent. This ideology is instrumental in convincing recruits and Muslim supporters that their actions are morally justifiable and required under Islamic law.

The NMSTP-WOT identifies extremist ideology as the strategic COG for the Al Qa'ida Associated Movement (AQAM). Further, it recognizes that each extremist network or organization will have different COGs from one another. What the NMSTP-WOT fails to understand is that the violence inherent and condoned by Islamic ideology cannot be separated by association from one group to another. It is the Muslim population support base that is empowered by Islamic ideology that the United States needs to focus on as the COG.

Safe havens:

Safe havens allow the enemy to conduct activities in support of their goals such as planning, organizing, recruiting, training, and conducting physical operations with minimal or no interference from opposing forces. These safe havens can be physical or non-physical and exist both in regulated and unregulated realms.

Physical safe havens exist in many forms. The most commonly known are state sponsored safe havens. In the GWOT, these state sponsored safe havens can exist where an established nation allows or encourages the religion of Islam. Iran, being an Islamic governed state, demonstrates one extreme spectrum of state sponsored safe havens. Iran has been actively supporting the violent spread of Islam by running state sponsored terrorist training camps. The rebirth of radical Islamic extremism can be traced back to Ayatollah Ruhollah Khomeini's rule and the strict Shia Islamic laws instituted throughout Iran.

Saudi Arabia is another state that encourages and supports the spread of Islam by providing safe havens for Islamic growth and education. Because Wahhabism is the state religion in Saudi Arabia, Wahhabist are allowed to preach and instruct the violent interpretations of the Qur'an. Though they may not have physical terrorist training camps, Saudi Arabia provides safe havens by funding, nurturing, and exporting Wahhabism throughout the world.

Currently, the United States could also be arguably considered a state sponsored safe haven for Islam. Civil rights and religious freedoms guaranteed by the United States Constitution and Bill of Rights allow many Islamic organizations and religious institutions to operate freely and ungoverned within United States borders. This includes subversive activities in mosques where it is legal, under the guise of freedom of religion, to preach and encourage the violent spread of Islam.

Other common physical safe havens include ungoverned or ill-governed space in state territories. These areas either have limited access by the ruling authorities or the ruling authorities posses no ability to physically govern. Somalia and the Philippines offer two examples of these safe havens. Somalia, though a state, has no functional government within its borders. Hence, several Islamic extremist groups have established functional training and operating bases there. The Philippines, though having a functional government, is so vast and inundated with small islands that it is virtually impossible to govern or regulate the Islamic activities taking place there.

Non-physical safe havens are virtual spaces that allow the enemy to conduct such tasks as organize, equip, and communicate. Cyber, financial, and legal systems are all examples of this realm. Each of these safe havens are equally difficult to regulate or monitor and provide the enemy the ability to function and perform their tasks relatively free from disruption.

Education:

Education is truly one of the critical capabilities of the support base of the world's Muslim movement. Education under the Wahhabi missionaries firmly reinforces the violent spread of Islam while simultaneously assisting in the recruitment and indoctrination of future Muslims around the world. Charities based out of Saudi Arabia continue to fund the spreading of Islamic fundamentalism through education. "The al Haramain Islamic Foundation, one such Saudi based charity, reportedly funded some

3000 Wahhabi missionaries and concentrated heavily in establishing new Wahhabi Mosques in Southeast Asia, the Balkans, and Africa."[51]

Madrassas are an instrumental part of Islamic education and recruitment of millions. An explosive growth in the number of Madrassas around the world has taken place due to Saudi wealth and Islamic charity contributions. Originally designed as seminaries, the Madrassas were utilized to educate students in reading and religious studies. In the 1980s, the Madrassas transformed into recruiting and organizing schools to fight the Soviet Union in Afghanistan. Islamic ideology was discovered to be an efficient tool in recruiting and creating an efficient guerilla army. The success of the Afghan Madrassas in recruiting and training religious fighters has been capitalized upon recently by the Islamic extremists. Madrassas being established around the world today promote curriculums that focus on a mixed dosage of Islam with a lot of military training, emphasizing the duty of Muslims to spread Islam by any means. These Madrassas throughout the world and in many developing nations are the only real opportunity for many young males to receive an education.

Recruitment grounds:

Another CC of the Muslim support base is the vast recruitment grounds of the world. The majority of these reside in poverty stricken third world countries with little or no governance. In these regions, the majority of targeted recruits are among the lower classes and peasants. These candidates provide an unlimited source of possible recruits who do not have any access to any other kind of schooling. Originating from mostly illiterate or ill-educated families, these students are highly susceptible to the violent Wahhabi ideology of Islam.

One of the most productive recruitment grounds for Islam is Asia. Already heavily populated with Muslims, the combination of poverty and isolation from governance make this region highly susceptible to Islamic ideology. For many years, "scholarships" funded by Saudi Arabia have been recruiting Central Asian, Filipino, and Indonesian students back to Saudi. There they are indoctrinated, educated, and raised in the Wahhabi school system. Many of these scholarship students are groomed to become preachers or teachers in Wahhabism, then retuned to their native countries to run their own mosque or Madrassa funded again through Saudi and other Islamic charities. The rapid growth of these institutions is filling a structured educational void in these isolated recruitment grounds and capitalizing on the illiterate population to increase the ranks of the Muslim support base.

Africa is another recruitment ground for the Muslim support base that is starting to show similar Wahhabi institutional growth to that taking place in Asia. Already influenced by Islam in the historical Caliphate, the Muslim roots in Africa are being re-cultivated by Wahhabism ideology backed by Saudi and Islamic funding. Decades of famine, drought, and war have resulted in Africa being one of the poorest continents on the planet. The combination of large youth populations, poverty, and illiteracy make this region a fertile recruitment ground for Wahhabi ideology.

The vastness of the regions additionally fosters many ungoverned or ill-governed space in the state territories. These areas have limited access by the ruling authorities or either the ruling authorities posses no ability to physically govern. The mosques and Madrassas in these areas are allowed to recruit, indoctrinate, educate, and train in any curriculum they deem appropriate. Islamic extremists are cultivating these sources to further their ranks and the spread of Islam. Vali Nasr supports this point by stating: "that's why the ideology that's propagated by these schools is so significant in shaping minds in the Muslim world. So if regular schooling is not schooling people, and schools that propagate fanaticism are schooling people, it doesn't take a brain surgeon to figure out what would be the impact on society."[52]

Acceptable social tolerance:

Acceptable social tolerance for violence and terrorism is another Critical Capability of the Muslim support base. The inherent violence of Islam is a reinforced byproduct of the Arab culture. Violence and war have historically been woven into the history of the Middle East and "Jihad has existed since the advent of Islam fourteen hundred years ago."[53] Islam has incorporated this violence into its ideology to justify and assist in the spreading of Islam. Violence and death for the cause of Islam are not only celebrated, but they are rewarded in the Islamic religion.

This cultural adaptation to violence has now evolved into acceptable social tolerance in the Muslim populations of the world. The images reported on TV of the celebrations taking place in many streets in the Middle East when the World Trade Towers collapsed on 9/11 are a visible example. These crowds massing in the streets in celebration of successful terrorist bombings are directly contributing to the terrorist cause. They are publicly condoning the actions and, at a minimum, providing the terrorists morale support and further popularity. Terrorists like Bin-Ladin and Zarqawi are extremely popular and celebrated as heroes among many Muslim populations. It is this popularity and support that provides the endless supply of willing terrorists. These terrorists are actively supporting the Islamic movement and represent the Islamic struggle against the United States.

Likewise, these violent actions and terrorist acts around the world are being condoned by the majority of the Muslim population. At the very least, their silent support is well noted. Thousands of Muslims staged violent protest throughout the world and burned President Bush in effigy over a cartoon depicting Mohammed. There were no apparent Muslim protests over the killing of 2752 civilians on 9/11. A few press releasements were made by Islamic clerics base in the United States condemning the 9/11 attacks, but I would suspect these statements were made more in the cause of self-preservation than as the voice of a remorseful Muslim population.

It is not a fact that all Muslims are violent, but the majority of them do support the violent actions taking place in the world, either directly or indirectly. The Islamic extremists "have achieved almost universal support for their goals in the Muslim community, because their ultimate message is an Islamic one, fight for Islam. It is a message that is impossible for a Muslim not to support."[54] Muslims must understand that by not openly condemning these violent actions, they are consenting by silence. If they truly believe in peace and condemn these violent actions, then it is their responsibility to police their own religion and stop supporting the Muslims who conduct these acts of violence.

Exploiting Critical Vulnerabilities:

To properly exploit the critical vulnerabilities of the Muslim support base, the entire spectrum of the United States elements of national power, DIME, must be brought to bear. Winning this Holy War will not be quick, and will require the coordination of all the elements of DIME to cripple the Muslim support base that is the COG. For the purpose of this discussion, critical vulnerabilities will be defined as "those aspects or components of critical capabilities that are deficient, or vulnerable to neutralization, interdiction, or attack in a manner achieving decisive or significant results, disproportionate to the military resources applied."[55] It should also be noted that these critical capabilities often overlap and will often share common critical vulnerabilities.

Finance CV:

Diplomatic and Economic elements of national power will be the two leading tools in attacking the critical capability of finance. The United States must encourage other nations to become more active in the monitoring of world banking institutions. These actions would include, but not be limited to, enforcing documentation of all financial transactions and making this information available to legitimate governments. Rogue banking systems that operate outside these parameters or intentionally fail to comply should be isolated from the rest of the banking world. A complete reorganization of the Saudi banking system under government control would be a good place to start.

Closer scrutinization of businesses and shell companies associated with known and suspected terrorist organizations should be encouraged nationally and through the UN. Countries that continue to maintain a liberal no-look policy should be sanctioned by both the United States and the UN.

Islamic charities, especially those residing in the United States, should be forced by law to have better accountability of where their donations and zakat are ending up and to what purpose they are serving. Heavy penalties, to include the closure of that charity and jail time, should be assessed to those charities that have been linked to violent Islamic groups.

The rapid growth of Islamic extremists into organized crime operations, especially illegal drug trade related, should be exploited by law enforcement by loosening Posse Comitatus regulations that would allow the support of the military. By linking these terrorists to the illegal drug industry, military assets, especially intelligence gathering assets, could provide national level assets in assisting the war on drugs as well as strengthening the homeland defense posture.

Ideology CV:

Islamic ideology will need to be countered through a vigilant Information Operation. There will be multiple target audiences and concepts to this plan. The first goal should be to try and explain that the violent spread of Islam is not morally justified under Islamic law. Despite historical references in the Qur'an, that type of behavior is not condoned or accepted in today's world. Co-opting leading Islamic religious figures is key to the success of this plan. Options to neutralize or marginalize Islamic religious leaders who pronounce the opposite message should be seriously entertained.

A message of tolerance should be the next goal. A similar tack of explaining that other religions may now be tolerated in today's world and that the historical ideology of killing them has become obsolete. Globalization and population migrations have made it virtually impossible for Islam to be the sole religion on earth, and therefore Muslims should learn to tolerate and live with others of different faiths. The same recommendation would apply in the co-opting of key Islamic religious leaders as mentioned in the previous paragraph.

The concept that a better life and prosperity on earth can be obtained by living peacefully is achievable without jeopardizing one's soul in the after life or heaven should be the next goal. This would additionally include the investment of creating an economy or lively hood for regions that are impoverished. The same recommendations would apply in the co-opting of key Islamic religious leaders as mentioned in the first paragraph.

The final goal of the Information Operation would be to let the world Muslim population know that they will be held accountable for the violence conducted under the guise of Islam. Examples should be made of countries such as Iran who openly support Islamic extremists and encourage violence in the name of Islam. Regime change by any means should be the first step. Send a clear message to the world that any governing body who is openly a proponent of terrorism and genocide will not be tolerated.

Here in the United States, religious freedoms and rights granted under the Constitution should be closely monitored, suspended or revoked for Muslims. This could include the right of free assembly and of speech. The monitoring of sermons being given in mosques should be allowed to protect against sedition and indirect incitement. Australia has already introduced such legislation to their House of Representatives and Senate in the form of the *Anti-Terrorism Bill 2005*.[56] The message that freedom of religion does not take precedence over freedom of life must be made clear to the Muslim population and that they will be held accountable for the violence conducted in the name of Islam.

Safe Havens CV:

Denying safe havens as a critical capability for Muslim support base would focus on three actions. The first would be to create new laws that restrict or amend old laws that allow these Islamic extremists and their Muslim support base to exist and operate freely in governed states. Laws that provide violent organizations and their supporters shelter from the very state they are at war with should be amended to remove that protection. The Austrailian *Anti-Terrorism Bill 2005* is an excellent example of how to accomplish this goal.

The next action would be to assist governments that are unable to govern their region due to vastness or lack of resources. This could be done with financial aid or with initial assistance from established military forces. United States military training teams could be available for initial training and support of these governments. Favorable military arms sales and loans could also be included in this action.

Presence would be the final action in denying many of these ungo verned safe havens to the Islamic extremist and their Muslim support base. Presence in this case does not have to infer a physical form. Many regions inaccessible by conventional means can be monitored by national assets on a scheduled or routine basis.

It would impossible to completely deny or eliminate safe havens entirely due to the vastness of many regions on earth, but limiting the number of safe havens available is a positive step in the Holy War.

Education CV:

Countering the Wahhabist educational system will additionally have positive affects on Islamic ideology and recruitment of Islamic extremists. Saudi Arabia is the primary conduit in which to attack this critical capability. The first step is to encourage

Muslim governments, like Saudi Arabia, to regulate and reform the Madrassas. This would not only entail curtailing the violent rhetoric associated with Wahhabism, but expanding the curriculum to mandates other than memorizing the Qur'an. The threat of withholding the financial support provided to the Wahhabist by the Saudi government would provide a relative incentive.

Another step in countering the Wahhabist educational system would be to compete with it with an alternative educational system. Led by the State Department, support and funding from religions other than Islam, as well as UN funded programs, could be invested in educational endeavors into the more desolate regions of the world. At the very least, this would help break the monopoly being established by the Wahhabist in 'at-risk' third world countries.

Recruitment Grounds CV:

Removing the advantage that the Muslim support base has in its ability to establish and benefit from recruitment grounds shares linkages with safe haven and educational critical vulnerabilities. One additional action that the United States could take to gain an advantage in this realm is establishing a new Combatant Command in Africa. The continent of Africa is proving to be a newly tapped source for both Islamic extremist and the Muslim population that supports them. By establishing an African Command (AFCOM), the United States would be addressing and countering several critical capabilities of the enemy at once. Presence, commitment, resolve, and reach would all be force multipliers and benefits of establishing an AFCOM.

Acceptable Social Tolerance CV:

The critical capabilities of this tenant are similar to those of ideology and therefore have similar vulnerabilities. The Information Operations conducted under the ideology campaign would have similar effects on the Muslim's acceptable social tolerance of violence and terrorism. The themes to be promulgated and reinforced would be that the violent spread of Islam is not morally justified under Islamic law, that tolerance of other religions should be accepted, and the concept that a better life and prosperity on earth can be obtained by living peacefully is achievable without jeopardizing one's soul in the after life or heaven. The final and most weighted tact would be to let the world Muslim population know that they will be held accountable for the violence conducted under the guise of Islam. Muslims must understand that by not openly condemning these violent actions, they are consenting by silence. If they truly believe in peace and condemn these violent actions, then it is their responsibility to police their own religion and stop supporting the Muslims who conduct these acts of violence.

A final theme in this proposed strategy is one of a coalition. The United States should attempt to continue to strengthen and recruit responsible governments of the world in this Holy War. Though the United States obviously has the lead in the GWOT, part of the new strategy should be to get the world to recognize that this is in fact a Holy War between Islam and the rest of the non-Muslim world. Prime candidates for this Global War On Islam (GWOI) would be those nations and states that are just beginning to recognize Islam and their Muslim support base as the true enemy. As Bernard Lewis points out, "Europe, more particularly Western Europe, is now home to a large and rapidly growing Muslim community, and many Europeans are beginning to see its presence as a problem, for some even a threat."[57]

Chapter 9.

APPEASEMENT

> There was never a war in all history easier to prevent by timely action than the
> one which has just desolated great areas of the globe. It could have been prevented
> without the firing of a single shot, but no one would listen.
> -Winston Churchill, 1950[58]

The United States' failure to correctly identify the religion of Islam and the Muslim population as the strategic enemy can be interpreted as a national policy of appeasement. The challenges and dilemmas that would arise from this confrontation may be too daunting and complex for any government. The combination of the large Muslim population, Saudi Arabian ties to Wahhabism, and the complexity of associated issues in acknowledging one's involvement in a Holy War may be too much for the United States administration. If appeasement of Islam and the Muslim population is in fact America's national strategy, lessons learned from previous national policies of appeasement should be examined to verify the validity of this strategy. The appeasement of Nazi Germany by the western governments during the 1930s and the subsequent outbreak of World War II offers a case-study with many similarities that can be applied to the current situation taking place with the religion of Islam and the Muslim population.

Hitler's remilitarization of the Rhineland in 1936 was justified, in his mind, as a rectification of the "injustices" of the Versailles Treaty following World War I. His continued strengthening of Germany's armed forces and his violent rhetoric threatened European peace and resulted in the Munich Conference of 1938. At this conference, Italy, Germany, France, and England began a strategy of appeasement to deter German aggression that might lead to war. The Sudetenland, with all its fortifications intact, was returned to Germany in exchange for Hitler's agreement that there would be no further

German conquest. Chamberlain, Mussolini, and Daladier all returned to their countries being hailed as peace-makers and credited with avoiding another world war.

These appeasements encouraged Hitler's beliefs that the European governments had lost their will to fight a major war; consequently, in March 1939, he invaded the remaining non-Germanic areas of Czechoslovakia. By carefully limiting Germany's explicit territorial demands to Germanic Europe under the guise of national self-determination, Hitler was able to further strengthen the German military without reprisal. European appeasement continued to fuel Hitler's conquests.

The Soviet Union demonstrated appeasement with Hitler when they entered a nonaggression pact with Germany in August 1939. This pact essentially freed German military forces to conduct attacks in the West with little fear of a war or second front on their East. A secret protocol contained in the nonaggression pact granted the Soviet Union the eastern half of Poland and conceded Finland, Estonia, and Latvia to Soviet determination unopposed by Germany.

French appeasement came in the form of the Maginot Line. Their military took no offensive action against Germany; instead, it awaited a German attack behind their defenses, resulting in the fall of France in June, 1940, following the German blitzkrieg.

The United States was practicing a policy of isolationism that precluded war or military alliance with threatened states in Europe.

For Great Britain, appeasement was about war avoidance consistent with preservation of their vital national interests. Great Britain failed to mobilize any substantial military land forces, instead banking on sufficient European continental allies to supply ground forces, thus limiting England's liability in a future war to the provision of naval and air power. The failure of European countries to take action in response to German aggression and further acts of appeasement towards Hitler established the foundations for the beginning of World War II.

The commonality between Hitler's Nazi Germany and Islam and their Muslim population support base can best be identified by looking at why appeasement failed to stop Hitler. Appeasement proved to be a misguided policy against Hitler for many of the same reasons appeasement would not work in America's current Holy War. The failure of Western European governments to grasp the nature of the Nazi regime and Hitler's strategic ambitions was instrumental in the failure of the appeasement policy. Appeasement failed because Hitler's goals were unappeasable. Hitler did not want to adjust the balance of power in Europe; rather, he intended to overthrow it and establish a German-ruled Europe. Islam shares the same characteristics in its view of religion. Islam does not want to merely spread the religion; it wants to establish it as the sole religion on earth. Islam embraces war for the same reason Hitler did: He knew he could not get what he wanted without it. Most states are unwilling to pay an exorbitant price for a chance at expansion; however, free of formal borders or of a governing body, Islam is more than willing to wage this Holy War. President George H.W. Bush clearly identified the faults of appeasement when dealing with aggression when he stated, "If history teaches anything, it is that we must resist aggression or it will destroy our freedoms. Appeasement does not work. As was the case in the 1930's, we see in Saddam Hussein an aggressive dictator threatening his neighbors."[59]

An extremely deep-rooted ideological belief is another common characteristic shared by Hitler and Islam. Hitler's ideology defined the scope of his territorial ambitions and the means in which he would take to achieve his goals. For Nazi Germany, revisionism of historic Germany was just an enabling prerequisite for a much larger agenda of racial enslavement and conquest. "Race, far from being a mere propagandistic slogan, was the very rock on which the Nazi Church was built," observes Norman Rich in his assessment of Hitler's war aims.[60] Many European leaders dismissed Hitler's ideological ranting on race as merely a domestic political platform. Yet in his book, Mein Kampf, Hitler clearly delineates his objects just as the Qur'an clearly states the goals of Islam. The spread of Islam by any means with the establishment of Islam as the sole religion on earth is the repeated theme. Islam's intentions are clearly stated just as Hitler's were, and they are being dismissed by the United States under appeasement, just like Hitler's were by the European governments.

Given Hitler's ideologically-driven expansionism and Islam's equal conviction of world dominance, a state (or religion) determined on war to achieve ideological objectives that cannot be obtained short of war is most unlikely to be susceptible to appeasement. Conversely, a state (or religion) seeking to avoid war and having limited objectives is more likely to be appeasable. Clearly, the religion of Islam, like Nazi Germany, falls into the first category. President George W. Bush was correct when talking of preventive war as a means of dealing with a rising enemy bent on domination. "Time is not on our side," he said in his 2002 State of the Union Address. "I will not wait on events while dangers gather. I will not stand by as peril draws closer and closer. The United States will not permit the world's most dangerous regimes to threaten us with the world's most dangerous weapons."[61] Unfortunately, given the Muslim population support base, the American preemptive attacks into Afghanistan and Iraq were not

enough to deter the Holy War taking place between the United States and Islam.
Germany rationalized the "injustices" of the Versailles Treaty to justify their actions;
likewise, the majority of Muslims rationalize their violence to counter the "injustices"
committed against Islam and Muslims by the West.

The lesson of the 1930s that appeasement seldom works and force should be used
early and decisively against rising security threats has been used by many United States
Presidents to justify decisions for war and military intervention. John F. Kennedy cited
the Munich analogy during the Cuban Missile Crises, warning that the "1930's taught us
a clear lesson: Aggressive conduct, if allowed to go unchecked, ultimately leads to
war."[62] Presidents Kennedy, Johnson, and Reagan have all demonstrated their
understanding that capitulating to the demands of an aggressor simply makes inevitable a
later and larger war on less favorable terms. By failing to name Islam and the Muslim
population support base as the strategic enemy, the United States administration is falling
into a policy of appeasement. The fortitude to hold a religion's faith responsible for their
members' actions is a huge task, yet one necessary to stem the violence of Islam and end
this Holy War.

Chapter 10.

Conclusion

The United States Administration faces a fundamental problem with critical implications of clearly defining the enemy. Trying to adequately describe who and what they are fighting without singling out one of the world's largest religious populations, Islam, as the true cause or facilitator of this Holy War is a dilemma that must be overcome. The violent overtones of Islam and their absolute ambitions for global dominance are evident. Given Islam's religious predisposition and cultural bias, the United States can no longer afford to interpret Islam as a peaceful religion. That strategic assumption will lead to America's defeat.

In the 20th century, Western democracy has defeated both Nazism and Communism. The 21st century's war will be one between Islam and Western Judeo/Christian civilizations. This Holy War will last until Islam gives up its ambitions for global dominance or Western civilization submits. Choosing to engage Islam now is the right course of action for the United States. Identifying Islam and the Muslim population support base as the strategic threat is no longer an option. The United States must adopt a strategy that correctly identifies the enemy, as well as correctly identifies and prosecutes the enemy's Center Of Gravity. Battle grounds like Iraq are a step in the right direction. Creating a democratic Iraq should provide a catalyst for democratic change in the rest of the Middle East.

Perhaps acknowledging or adopting a policy that identifies Islam as the threat is what the enemy wants, but the United States needs to draw the line or at least make sure the enemy knows that America is committed to victory no matter how large the obstacle.

If America chooses to ignore the true threat, she will eventually have to fight a much larger Islamic body who could not only encompass Europe, but possibly be armed with nuclear weapons.

There are prominent voices from the Muslim community as Bernard Lewis points out, who continue to say "how these radical fundamentalists-specifically extremist groups such as Al-Qa'ida; the preemptive fundamentalism of the Saudi establishment; and the institutionalized revolution of the ruling Iranian hierarchy-have hijacked Islam quite succinctly."[63] These Muslims insist that these groups and other radical fundamentalist are exploiting their interpretation of Islam for wrongful violence. I would argue that these Muslim voices defending Islam and trying to separate themselves from the violence and extremists are highly educated people and themselves a minority in the Muslim population. That they are in fact out of touch with the reality of the Holy War taking place between Islam and the West.

Is every Muslim in the world directly supporting the Holy War against America? The obvious answer is no. However, the Muslim population as a whole must understand that they will be held accountable for the violence conducted under the guise of Islam. They must be responsible as a community to police their own religion and stop supporting the Muslims who conduct these acts of violence or else the entire Muslim population will suffer. Muslims must further understand that by not openly condemning these violent actions, they are consenting by silence. The Muslim community must recognize the immense harm the Islamist violence has brought to their hopes of a better, more secure life; furthermore, without reform, that they will meet the same fate of both Nazism and Communism.

ENDNOTES

[1] "Muslim Population Worldwide." Islamic Population, 31 Dec 2005. http://www.islamicpopulatin.com/ accessed on 28 Feb 06.

[2] "Muslim Population Statistics." Muslim Population Statistics. http://muslim-canada.org/muslimstats.html accessed on 28 Feb 06.

[3] Friedman, Thomas, L. (2005). The World Is Flat . New York: Farrar, Straus and Giroux. pg 392.

[4] Friedman, Thomas, L. (2005). The World Is Flat . New York: Farrar, Straus and Giroux. pg 400.

[5] Friedman, Thomas, L. (2005). The World Is Flat . New York: Farrar, Straus and Giroux. pg 403.

[6] "Global War on Terrorism: Understanding the Long-Term Strategy-Why Education is key-." BG Robert L. Caslen Jr., J5, Deputy Director for War on Terrorism. 3 Feb 05. Derived from National Defense University, JFSC, JAWS student guide. Norfolk, Virginia September 2005.

[7] "President Addresses Military families, Discusses War on terror." President Bush. Idaho Center, Nampa, Idaho. Aug 05. The White House http://www.whitehouse.gov/news/releases/2005/08/html accessed on 24 Aug 05.

[8] GLOBAL WAR ON TERRORISM: ANALYZING THE STRATEGIC THREAT, Discussion Paper Number Thirteen, pg.132. Joint Military Intelligence College. November 2004.

[9] National Military Strategic Plan for the War on Terrorist. 1FEB2006. Chairman of the Joint Chiefs of Staff, Washington, DC 20318. pg 9.

[10] Carl von Clausewitz, On War, trans. Michael Howard and Peter Paret (New York: Knopf, 1993), pg 152.

[11] National Military Strategic Plan for the War on Terrorist. 1FEB2006. Chairman of the Joint Chiefs of Staff, Washington, DC 20318. pg 35.

[12] Merriam-Webster's Collegiate Dictionary, Eleventh Edition. (Springfield, Mass: Merriam-Webster, Incorporated, 2003), pg 594.

[13] National Military Strategic Plan for the War on Terrorist. 1FEB2006. Chairman of the Joint Chiefs of Staff, Washington, DC 20318. pg 18.

[14] "Address to a Joint Session of Congress and the American People." President Bush. United States Capitol, Washington, D.C. Sept 01. The White House http://www.whitehouse.gov/news/releases/2001/09/html accessed on 30 Nov 05.

[15] Ergun Mehmet Caner and Emir Fethi Caner, Unveiling Islam. Kregel publications, Grand Rapids, MI, 49501, 2002, pg 78.

[16] "Ruhollah Khomeini." Wikipedia, the free encyclopedia. http://www.wikipedia.com accessed on 24 Oct 05.

[17] "Text of Fatwah Urging Jihad Against Americans". World Islamic Front Statement, Published in Al-Quds al-'Arabi on February 23, 1998. http://www.ict.org.il/articles/fatwah.htm accessed on 24 Oct 05.

[18] "Text of Fatwah Urging Jihad Against Americans". Published in Al-Quds al-'Arabi on February 23, 1998. http://www.ict.org.il/articles/fatwah.htm accessed on 24 Oct 05.

[19] "Text of Fatwah Urging Jihad Against Americans". World Islamic Front Statement, Published in Al-Quds al-'Arabi on February 23, 1998. http://www.ict.org.il/articles/fatwah.htm accessed on 24 Oct 05.

[20] "Translation of April 24, 2002 al-Qaeda document". Middle East Policy Council Journal. 24 April 2002. http://www.mepc.org/public_asp/journal/vol10/0306_alqaeda.asp accessed on 21 Sept 05.

[21] "Translation of April 24, 2002 al-Qaeda document". Middle East Policy Council Journal. 24 April 2002. http://www.mepc.org/public_asp/journal/vol10/0306_alqaeda.asp accessed on 21 Sept 05.

[22] "Translation of April 24, 2002 al-Qaeda document". Middle East Policy Council Journal. 24 April 2002. http://www.mepc.org/public_asp/journal/vol10/0306_alqaeda.asp accessed on 21 Sept 05.

[23] "Osama bin Laden's Speech on the Eve of the 2004 US Elections". The Middle East Media Research Institute. 29 October 2004. http://www.memritv.org/Transcript.asp?P1=312 accessed on 8 Mar 05.

[24] "Osama bin Laden's Speech on the Eve of the 2004 US Elections". The Middle East Media Research Institute. 29 October 2004. http://www.memritv.org/Transcript.asp?P1=312 accessed on 8 Mar 05.

[25] Febe Armanios, Islam: Sunnis and Shiites, CRS Report for Congress. Congressional Research service, The Library of Congress, 23 February, 2004. pg 5.

[26] Col. Norvell b. de Atkin, USA Ret., "Islam, Islamism And Terrorism". ARMY; The Magazine of the Association of the United States Army, January 2006. pg 60.

[27] Andrew Coulson, <u>Education and Indoctrination in the Muslim World, Executive Summary</u>. Policy Analysis, CATO Institute, 11 March, 2004. pg 10.

[28] Loretta Napoleoni, "The Saudis: Friends or Foes?." The Progress Report, Special Guest Article. http://www.progress.org/2003/saudi01.htm accessed on 28 Feb 06. pg 1.

[29] Loretta Napoleoni, "The Saudis: Friends or Foes?." The Progress Report, Special Guest Article. http://www.progress.org/2003/saudi01.htm accessed on 28 Feb 06. pg 2.

[30] Mehdi Bozorgmehr and Anny Bakalin, "Closure of Muslim Philanthropic Organizations after 9/11". Middle East and Middle Eastern American Center, City University of New York. http://www.Web.gc.cuny.edu/memeac/research/closure_of_Muslim_Philanthropies.pdf accessed on 1 Mar 06.

[31] Jeremy Lippart and Kamran Bokhari, "The Finances of Terrorism", StratFor Weekly, 22 October, 2004. http://www.strafor.biz/produts/premium/read_artilce.php?selected=Terrorism accessed on 25 Jan 06.

[32] Ergun Mehmet Caner and Emir Fethi Caner, <u>More Than a Prophet</u>. 2003. Kregel publications, Grand Rapids, MI, 49501, 2002, pg 218.

[33] Ergun Mehmet Caner and Emir Fethi Caner, <u>Unveiling Islam</u>. Kregel publications, Grand Rapids, MI, 49501, 2002, pg 117-118.

[34] Ergun Mehmet Caner and Emir Fehi Caner, <u>Unveiling Islam.</u> Kregel publications, Grand Rapids, MI, 49501, 2002, pg 118.

[35] Ergun Mehmet Caner and Emir Fethi Caner, <u>Unveiling Islam.</u> Kregel publications, Grand Rapids, MI, 49501, 2002, pg 49.

[36] National Military Strategic Plan for the War on Terroris. 1FEB2006. Chairman of the Joint Chiefs of Staff, Washington, DC 20318. pg 4.

[37] Col. Norvell B. De Atkine, USA Ret., Islam, Islamism And Terrorism. <u>ARMY; The Magazine of the Association of the United States Army</u>, January 2006. pg 58.

[38] National Military Strategic Plan for the War on Terrorist. 1FEB2006. Chairman of the Joint Chiefs of Staff, Washington, DC 20318. pg 21.

[39] Ergun Mehmet Caner and Emir Fethi Caner, <u>More Than a Prophet</u>. 2003. Kregel publications, Grand Rapids, MI, 49501, 2002, pg 219.

[40] Joint Operation Planning, Revision Third Draft (3), 10 August 2005. Joint Publication 5-0. pg IV-10.

[41] Rear Admiral Bill Sullivan, "Fighting the Long War—Military Strategy for the War on Terrorism" Vice Director for Strategic Plans & Policy, The Joint Staff. Executive Lecture Forum, Radvanyi Chair in International Security Studies, Mississippi State University. Slide #6.

[42] Loretta Napoleoni, "The Saudis: Friends or Foes?." The Progress Report, Special Guest Article. http://www.progress.org/2003/saudi01.htm accessed on 28 Feb 06. pg 2.

[43] "Second Report of the Monitoring Group Established Pursuant to United Nations Security Council Resolution 1363 (2001) and extended by resolutions 1390 (2002) and 1455 (2003) on sanctions against Al Qaqeda, S/2003/1070, December 3, 2003, para 68.

[44] "Philippine Country Report, UN Security Council Resolution 1267 and 1455, Al Qaeda Sanctions Committee, October, 2004 S/AC.37/2003 /(1455)/79, October 22, 2003.

[45] Victor Comras, "Al Qaeda Finances and Funding to Affiliated Group", <u>Strategic Insights, Volume IV, Issue 1 January 2005</u>. Naval Postgraduate School, Monterey, Cal. http://www.ccc.nps.navy.mil/si/2005/Jan/comrasJan05.asp assessed on 28 Feb 06.

[46] "Second Report of the Monitoring Group Established Pursuant to United Nations Security Council Resolution 1363 (2001) and extended by resolutions 1390 (2002) and 1455 (2003) on sanctions against Al Qaqeda, S/2003/1070, December 3, 2003

[47] "Interview with Mr. Mirwas Yasini head of the Counter Narcotic Directorate (CND) Kabul." IRIN News Service, October 19, 2004.

[48] Anonymous. <u>Through Our Enemies' Eyes</u>, Washington, DC: Brassey', Inc., 2002. pg 29.

[49] Anonymous. <u>Through Our Enemies' Eyes</u>, Washington, DC: Brassey', Inc., 2002. pg 29.

[50] Lewis, Bernard (2003). <u>The Crisis of Islam: unholy War and Holy Terror</u>. New York: Random House Publishing, Inc. pg 133.

[51] Victor Comras, "Al Qaeda Finances and Funding to Affiliated Group", <u>Strategic Insights, Volume IV, Issue 1 January 2005</u>. Naval Postgraduate School, Monterey, Cal. http://www.ccc.nps.navy.mil/si/2005/Jan/comrasJan05.asp assessed on 28 Feb 06.

[52] Vali Nasr as interviewed by Richard Holbrooke. "Analysis Madrassas", Frontline, PBS. 25 October 2001. http://www.pbs.org/wgbh/pages/frontline/shows/saudi/analyses/madrassas.html assessed on 8 Mar 06.

[53] GLOBAL WAR ON TERRORISM: ANALYZING THE STRATEGIC THREAT, Discussion Paper Number Thirteen, p.125. Joint Military Intelligence College. November 2004.

[54] GLOBAL WAR ON TERRORISM: ANALYZING THE STRATEGIC THREAT, Discussion Paper Number Thirteen, pg 53. Joint Military Intelligence College. November 2004

[55] Joint Operation Planning, Revision Third Draft (3), 10 August 2005. Joint Publication 5-0. pg IV-13.

[56] "Anti-Terrorism Bill 2005, No. , 2005. Attorney-General, The Parliament of the Commonwealth of Australia, House of Representatives/The Senate. Draft-In-Confidence. B05PG201.v28.doc 7/10/2005

[57] Lewis, Bernard. The Crisis of Islam: unholy War and Holy Terror. New York: Random House Publishing, Inc. 2003, pg 134.

[58] See Robert J. Young, "French Military Intelligence and Nazi Germany. 1938-1939," in Ernest R. May, ed., Knowing One's Enemies, op. cit.c pg. 271-309.

[59] Address to the nation announcing the deployment of United States armed forces to Saudi Arabia, August 8, 1990, George H.W. Bush, Public Papers of the Presidents of the United States: George Bush 1990, Washington, DC: U.S. Government Printing Office, 1991, II, p. 108.

[60] Norman Rich, Hitler's War aims: Ideology, the Nazi State, and the Course of Expansion, New York: W.W. Norton, 1973, pg. 4.

[61] George W. Bush, State of the Union Address, January 29, 2002. http://www.whitehouse.gov/news/releases/2002/01/print/20020129-11.html. Accessed on 30 Nov 05.

[62] Quoted in Theodore C. Sorenson, Kennedy, New York: Harper and Row, 1965, p.703.

[63] Lewis, Bernard. The Crisis of Islam: unholy War and Holy Terror. New York: Random House Publishing, Inc. (2003). pg 138.

BIBLIOGRAPHY

"Address to a Joint Session of Congress and the American People." President Bush. United States Capitol, Washington, D.C. Sept 01. The White House http://www.whitehouse.gov/news/releases/2001/09/html (accessed on 30 Nov 05).

Anonymous. Through Our Enemies' Eyes. Washington, DC: Brassey', Inc., 2002, 29.

"Anti-Terrorism Bill 2005, No., 2005. Attorney-General, The Parliament of the Commonwealth of Australia, House of Representatives/The Senate." Draft-In-Confidence. B05PG201.v28.doc 7/10/2005.

Armanios, Febe. Islam: Sunnis and Shiites, CRS Report for Congress. Congressional Research service, The Library of Congress, 23 February, 2004, 5.

Bozorgmehr, Mehdi and Anny Bakalin. "Closure of Muslim Philanthropic Organizations after 9/11." Middle East and Middle Eastern American Center, City University of New York. http://www.Web.gc.cuny.edu/memeac/research/closure_of_Muslim_Philanthropies.pdf (accessed on 1 Mar 06).

Bush, George H.W. "Public Papers of the Presidents of the United States: George Bush 1990." Washington, DC: U.S. Government Printing Office, 1991, II, 108.

Bush, George W. "President Addresses Military families, Discusses War on terror." Idaho Center, Nampa, Idaho. Aug 05. The White House http://www.whitehouse.gov/news/releases/2005/08/html (accessed on 24 Aug 05).

Bush, George W. "State of the Union Address." January 29, 2002. http://www.whitehouse.gov/news/releases/2002/01/print/20020129-11.html. (accessed on 30 Nov 05).

Caner, Ergun Mehmet and Emir Fethi Caner. More Than a Prophet. 2003. Grand Rapids: Kregel publications, 2002, 218-219.

Caner, Ergun Mehmet and Emir Fethi Caner. Unveiling Islam. Grand Rapids: Kregel publications, 2002, 49, 78, 117-118.

Comras, Victor. "Al Qaeda Finances and Funding to Affiliated Group," Strategic Insights, Volume IV, Issue 1 January 2005. Naval Postgraduate School, Monterey, Cal. http://www.ccc.nps.navy.mil/si/2005/Jan/comrasJan05.asp (assessed on 28 Feb 06).

Coulson, Andrew, Education and Indoctrination in the Muslim World, Executive Summary. Policy Analysis, CATO Institute, 11 March, 2004, 10.

De Atkine, Norvell B., Col, USA Ret. "Islam, Islamism And Terrorism." <u>ARMY: The Magazine of the Association of the United States Army</u>, January 2006, 58,60.

Friedman, Thomas L. <u>The World Is Flat</u>. 2005. New York: Farrar, Straus and Giroux publications.

"Global War on Terrorism: Analyzing the Strategic Threat," Discussion Paper Number Thirteen, 53,125,132. Joint Military Intelligence College. November 2004.

"Global War on Terrorism: Understanding the Long-Term Strategy-Why Education is key-." BG Robert L. Caslen Jr., J5, Deputy Director for War on Terrorism. 3 Feb 05. Derived from National Defense University, JFSC, JAWS student guide. Norfolk, Virginia September 2005.

Herzstein, Robert, Edwin. <u>Adolf Hitler and the German Trauma, 1913-1945, An Interpretation Of The Nazi Phenomenon</u>. 1974. New York: Capricorn Books.

Joint Operation Planning, Revision Third Draft (3), 10 August 2005. Joint Publication 5-0, IV-10, IV-13.

Lecture Forum, Radvanyi Chair in International Security Studies, Mississippi State University, Slide #6.

Lewis, Bernard. <u>The Crisis of Islam: unholy War and Holy Terror.</u> 2003. New York: Random House Publishing, Inc., 133-134, 138.

Lippart, Jeremy and Kamran Bokhari. "The Finances of Terrorism," StratFor Weekly, 22 October, 2004. http://www.strafor.biz/produts/premium/read_artilce.php?selected=Terrorism (accessed on 25 Jan 06).

<u>Merriam-Webster's Collegiate Dictionary</u>, Eleventh Edition. Springfield, Mass: Merriam-Webster, Incorporated, 2003, 594.

Millet, Allen R. and Murray, William. <u>Calculations, Net Assessment and the Coming of World War II</u>. 1992. New York: The Free Press.

"Muslim Population Worldwide." Islamic Population, 31 Dec 2005. http://www.islamicpopulatin.com/ (accessed on 28 Feb 06).

"Muslim Population Statistics." Muslim Population Statistics. http://muslim-canada.org/muslimstats.html (accessed on 28 Feb 06).

Napoleoni, Loretta. "The Saudis: Friends or Foes ?." The Progress Report, Special Guest Article. http://www.progress.org/2003/saudi01.htm (accessed on 28 Feb 06), 1-2.

Nasr, Vali. Interviewed by Richard Holbrooke. "Analysis Madrassas," Frontline, PBS. 25 October 2001. http://www.pbs.org/wgbh/pages/frontline/shows/saudi/analyses/madrassas.html (assessed on 8 Mar 06).

National Military Strategic Plan for the War on Terrorist. 1FEB2006. Chairman of the Joint Chiefs of Staff, Washington, DC 20318, 4, 18, 9, 21, 35.

"Osama bin Laden's Speech on the Eve of the 2004 US Elections." The Middle East Media Research Institute. 29 October 2004. http://www.memritv.org/Transcript.asp?P1=312 (accessed on 8 Mar 05).

"Osama bin Laden's Speech on the Eve of the 2004 US Elections." The Middle East Media Research Institute. 29 October 2004. http://www.memritv.org/Transcript.asp?P1=312 (accessed on 8 Mar 05).

"Philippine Country Report, UN Security Council Resolution 1267 and 1455, Al Qaeda Sanctions Committee," October, 2004 S/AC.37/2003/(1455)/79, October 22, 2003.

Rich, Norman. Hitler's War aims: Ideology, the Nazi State, and the Course of Expansion, New York: W.W. Norton, 1973, 4.

Rock, Wlliam R. British Appeasement in the 1930s. New York: W.W. Norton & Company, Inc., 1977.

"Ruhollah Khomeini." Wikipedia, the free encyclopedia. http://www.wikipedia.com (accessed on 24 Oct 05).

"Second Report of the Monitoring Group Established Pursuant to United Nations Security Council Resolution 1363 (2001) and extended by resolutions 1390 (2002) and 1455 (2003) on sanctions against Al Qaqeda, S/2003/1070," December 3, 2003, para 68.

Sorenson, Theodore C. Kennedy. New York: Harper and Row, 1965, 703.

Sullivan, Bill Rear Admiral. "Fighting the Long War—Military Strategy for the War on Terrorism" Vice Director for Strategic Plans & Policy, The Joint Staff. Executive Lecture Forum, Radvanyi Chair in International Security Studies, Mississippi State University, Slide #6.

"Text of Fatwah Urging Jihad Against Americans." World Islamic Front Statement, Published in Al-Quds al-'Arabi on February 23, 1998. http://www.ict.org.il/articles/fatwah.htm (accessed on 24 Oct 05).

"Translation of April 24, 2002 al-Qaeda document." Middle East Policy Council Journal. 24 April 2002. http://www.mepc.org/public_asp/journal/vol10/0306_alqaeda.asp (accessed on 21 Sept 05).

Von Clausewitz, Carl. On War, trans. Michael Howard and Peter Paret. New York: Knopf, 1993, 152.

Yasini, Mirwas. "Interview with Mr. Mirwas Yasini, head of the Counter Narcotic Directorate (CND) Kabul." IRIN News Service, October 19, 2004.

Young, Robert J. "French Military Intelligence and Nazi Germany. 1938-1939," quoted in Ernest R. May, ed., Knowing One's Enemies, op. cit.c, 271-309.

BIOGRAPHY

Lieutenant Colonel Parker graduated from The Citadel in May 1986, he was commissioned a Second Lieutenant through the Platoon Leader's Class (PLC) Program.
He reported to The Basic School for active duty in June 1986. Following The Basic School and completion of flight training in Pensacola, Florida, LtCol Parker was designated an Unrestricted Naval Aviator in July 1987. He then reported to HMMT-204, MCAS New River, North Carolina for training as a CH-46E Pilot.

LtCol Parker completed his first fleet assignment with the Blue Eagles of HMM-263 from 1989 to 1994. Major deployments included Operations Desert Shield/Desert Storm and Operation Eastern Exit, the evacuation of the American Embassy in Somalia, with 4th Marine Expeditionary Brigade. He participated in Operation Restore Hope and Operation Continue Hope in Somalia, and Operations Cease Fire in the Red Sea and Persian Gulf with the 24th Marine Expeditionary Unit (Special Operations Capable). Additional deployments included operations in Norway, Grenada, and several Caribbean locations. His duties include assignments as Assistant Maintenance Officer, Operations Officer, and Squadron Weapons and Tactics Officer.

In February 1994, LtCol Parker reported to 2DBn/4th Marines, Camp Lejeune, NC. LtCol Parker remained with the Battalion when they were re-designated as 2DBn/6th Marines and deployed with the Battalion in support of Operation Sea Signal under JTF-160. Battalion assignments included Assistant Operations Officer and Battalion Air Officer. In August 1995, he attended the Amphibious Warfare School in Quantico VA.

In May 1996, LtCol Parker reported to HMM-365, MCAS New River, North Carolina. As a Blue Knight, he served as Maintenance Officer and Operations Officer for two separate deployment cycles. Major deployments included Operation Joint Endeavor (Adriatic Sea), Operation Silverwake (Non-combatant Evacuation Operation in Albania), and Operation Guardian Retrieval (Congo/Zaire, Africa) with the 26th MEU (SOC). LtCol Parker participated in Operations Allied Force and Allied Harbour, Operation JTF Shining Hope (Macedonia), Operation Noble Anvil, Operation Joint Guardian (Kosovo), and Operation Avid Response (Turkey) with the 24th MEU (SOC).

In November 1999, LtCol Parker attended the College of Naval Command and Staff at the Naval War College, Newport, Rhode Island, where he earned a Masters of Arts Degree in National Security and Strategic Studies.

In November 2000, LtCol Parker reported to COMNAVAIRLANT as the Type Commander and Rotary Wing Class Desk for all AIRLANT rotary wing aircraft. He then reported to MAG-26 in July 2003 and assumed the duties as the Executive Officer, Marine Medium Helicopter Squadron 261 in October 2003.

Lieutenant Colonel Parker assumed command of HMM-261, 30 April 2004, in Al Asad Air Base, Iraq. While serving as Commanding Officer, provided medium lift assault support to I MEF and 3D MAW combat operations in support of USCOMCENTCOM during Operation Iraqi Freedom II to include Operation Vigilant Resolve, Al Fallujah, IZ. Under his command, the unit had no casualties and zero loss of aircraft.

LtCol Parker is currently attending the Joint Advanced Warfighting School (JAWS), JFSC, Norfolk, Va.

LtCol Parker's personal decorations include the Bronze Star, Meritorious Service Medal (with Gold Star), Strike Flight and Mission Air Medals, the Navy and Marine Corps Commendation

Medal, the Navy and Marine Corps Achievement Medal, and the Combat Action Ribbon (with Gold Star).